The Teachings of Confucius

By
Confucius
&
Daniel Willey

Copyright © 2014 Daniel Willey
All Rights Reserved

This book contains material protected under International and Federal Copyright Laws and Treaties. Any unauthorized reprint or use of this material is prohibited. No part of this book may be reproduced or transmitted in any form or by any means, electronic or mechanical, including photocopying, recording, or by any information storage or retrieval system without express written permission from the author.

ISBN-13: 978-1495370342
ISBN-10: 1495370348

All rights reserved.
Published by Easy Publishing Company
http://www.easypublishingcompany.com
contact@easypublishingcompany.com
Salt Lake City, UT 84108

First Edition: January 2014
Printed in the United States of America

Table of Contents

Ways to Use this Book	4
Introduction	5
10 Most Popular Teachings	6
Ability	9
Alertness	10
Anger & Blame	11
Character	12
Failures, Mistakes, & Flaws	20
Friends & Friendship	23
Goals	24
Habits	25
Happiness	26
Heart & Love	29
How to Live	31
Humility	40
Influence	41
Intelligence	43
Knowledge & Learning	44
Personal Development	48
Revenge	50
Truth	51
Uniqueness	53
Virtue	54
More by the Author	58
About the Author	59

Ways to Use this Book:

1. Start your day by reading a quote. Start at the front and read one quote per day. Write the quote down and share it throughout your day with others.
2. Buy a journal and record your responses to each of the quotes. Write down your feelings, thoughts, and inspirations.
3. Read this book as you would read any other book, from beginning to end.

Introduction

Confucius was a Chinese teacher, editor, politician, and philosopher of the Spring and Autumn period of Chinese history. The philosophy of Confucius emphasized personal and governmental morality, correctness of social relationships, justice and sincerity. His followers competed successfully with many other schools during the Hundred Schools of Thought era only to be suppressed in favor of the Legalists during the Qin Dynasty. Following the victory of Han over Chu after the collapse of Qin, Confucius's thoughts received official sanction and were further developed into a system known as Confucianism.

I have always considered quotes to be a very valuable asset to my inspiration. For years I have scoured the web to find meaningful quotes from inspirational people. When I find an especially meaningful quote, I love to share it with those close to me. I think that when you share something special to yourself, it can become even more meaningful and help out others.

NOTE: The Quotes in this book are collected from many sources and time periods. To respect the integrity of the authors' work, I have made every reasonable effort to correctly attribute each quote to the original author, but in a few cases it was impossible to find the exact original quote.

The 10 Most Popular Teachings of Confucius

"Choose a job you love, and you will never have to work a day in your life."

"Everything has beauty, but not everyone sees it."

"I hear and I forget. I see and I remember. I do and I understand."

"If I am walking with two other men, each of them will serve as my teacher. I will pick out the good points of the one and imitate them, and the bad points of the other and correct them in myself."

"It does not matter how slowly you go as long as you do not stop."

"Men's natures are alike, it is their habits that carry them far apart."

"No matter where you go – there you are"

"Our greatest glory is not in never falling, but in getting up every time we do."

"Wherever you go, go with all your heart."

"Worry not that no one knows of you; seek to be worth knowing."

Ability

"Ability will never catch up with the demand for it."

"The expectations of life depend upon diligence; the mechanic that would perfect his work must first sharpen his tools."

Alertness

"The superior man, when resting in safety, does not forget that danger may come."

"When in a state of security he does not forget the possibility of ruin. When all is orderly, he does not forget that disorder may come. Thus his person is not endangered, and his States and all their clans are preserved."

Anger and Blame

"If a man be under the influence of anger his conduct will not be correct."

"It was by music that the ancient kings gave elegant expression to their joy. By their armies and axes they gave the same to their anger."

"To be wronged is nothing unless you continue to remember it."
"When anger rises, think of the consequences."

Character

"Earnest in practicing the ordinary virtues, and careful in speaking about them, if, in his practice, he has anything defective, the superior man dares not but exert himself; and if, in his words, he has any excess, he dares not allow himself such license."

"Faced with what is right, to leave it undone shows a lack of courage."

"Forget injuries, never forget kindnesses."

"Great as heaven and earth are, men still find some things in them with which to be dissatisfied. Thus it is that, were the superior man to speak of his way in all its greatness, nothing in the world would be found able to embrace it, and were he to speak of it in its minuteness, nothing in the world would be found able to split it."

"Hold faithfulness and sincerity as first principles. Then no friends would not be like yourself."

"I will not be concerned at other men's not knowing me; I will be concerned at my own want of ability."

"In archery we have something like the way of the superior man. When the archer misses the center of the target, he turns round and seeks for the cause of his failure in himself."

"It is easy to hate and it is difficult to love. This is how the whole scheme of things works. All good things are difficult to achieve; and bad things are very easy to get."

"Look at the means which a man employs, consider his motives, observe his pleasures. A man simply cannot conceal himself!"

"Never give a sword to a man who can't dance."

"Only the wisest and stupidest of men never change."

"Respect yourself and others will respect you."

"Sincerity is that whereby self-completion is effected, and its way is that by which man must direct himself."

"The man who in view of gain thinks of righteousness; who in the view of danger is prepared to give up his life; and who does not forget an old agreement however far back it extends – such a man may be reckoned a complete man."

"The superior man acts before he speaks, and afterwards speaks according to his action."

"The superior man cannot be known in little matters, but he may be entrusted with great concerns. The small man may not be entrusted with great concerns, but he may be known in little matters."

"The superior man has nothing to compete for. But if he must compete, he does it in an archery match, wherein he ascends to his position, bowing in deference. Descending, he drinks the ritual cup."

"The superior man is all-embracing and not partial. The inferior man is partial and not all-embracing."

"The superior man is aware of Righteousness, the inferior man is aware of advantage."

"There is nothing more visible than what is secret, and nothing more manifest than what is minute. Therefore the superior man is watchful over himself, when he is alone."

"What the superior man seeks is in himself; what the small man seeks is in others."

"Wisdom, compassion, and courage are the three universally recognized moral qualities of men."

"Without an acquaintance with the rules of propriety, it is impossible for the character to be established."

"Without feelings of respect, what is there to distinguish men from beasts?"

Failure, Mistakes, and Flaws

"A man who has committed a mistake and doesn't correct it is committing another mistake."

"Be not ashamed of mistakes and thus make them crimes."

"Better a diamond with a flaw than a pebble without."

"If you make a mistake, do not be afraid to correct it."

"In all things success depends on previous preparation, and without such previous preparation there is sure to be failure."

"The cautious seldom err."

"The faults of a superior man are like the sun and moon. They have their faults, and everyone sees them; they change and everyone looks up to them."

"Things that are done, it is needless to speak about … things that are past, it is needless to blame."

"When you have faults, do not fear to abandon them."

Friends and Friendship

"I do not want a friend who smiles when I smile, who weeps when I weep, for my shadow in the pool can do better than that."

"It is more shameful to distrust our friends than to be deceived by them."

"Never contract friendship with a man that is not better than thyself."

"Silence is a true friend who never betrays."

Goals

"When it is obvious that the goals cannot be reached, don't adjust the goals, adjust the action steps."

Habits

"To practice five things under all circumstances constitutes perfect virtue; these five are gravity, generosity of soul, sincerity, earnestness, and kindness."

Happiness

"If a man has no humaneness what can his propriety be like? If a man has no humaneness what can his happiness be like?"

"If a man takes no thought about what is distant, he will find sorrow near at hand."

"The superior man is satisfied and composed; the mean man is always full of distress."

"The wise find pleasure in water; the virtuous find pleasure in hills. The wise are active; the virtuous are tranquil. The wise are joyful; the virtuous are long-lived."

"They must often change who would be constant in happiness or wisdom."

"We should feel sorrow, but not sink under its oppression."

"With coarse rice to eat, with water to drink, and my bended arm for a pillow – I have still joy in the midst of these things. Riches and honors acquired by unrighteousness are to me as a floating cloud."

Heart and Love

"Can there be a love which does not make demands on its object?"

"If you look into your own heart, and you find nothing wrong there, what is there to worry about? What is there to fear?"

"Recompense injury with justice, and recompense kindness with kindness."

"The superior man examines his heart, that there may be nothing wrong there, and that he may have no cause for dissatisfaction with himself. That wherein the superior man cannot be equaled is simply this — his work which other men cannot see."

How to Live

"Although your father and mother are dead, if you propose to yourself any good work, only reflect how it will make their names illustrious, and your purpose will be fixed."

"At fifteen my heart was set on learning; at thirty I stood firm; at forty I had no more doubts; at fifty I knew the mandate of heaven; at sixty my ear was obedient; at seventy I could follow my heart's desire without transgressing the norm."

"Being in humaneness is good. If we select other goodness and thus are far apart from humaneness, how can we be the wise?"

""Consideration for others is the basic of a good life, a good society."

"Death and life have their determined appointments; riches and honors depend upon heaven."

"Do not impose on others what you yourself do not desire."
"He who will not economize will have to agonize."

"How great is the path proper to the Sage! Like overflowing water, it sends forth and nourishes all things, and rises up to the height of heaven. All-complete is its greatness! It embraces the three hundred rules of ceremony, and the three thousand rules of demeanor. It waits for the proper man, and then it is trodden. Hence it is said, 'Only by perfect virtue can the perfect path, in all its courses, be made a fact.'"

"I want you to be everything that's you, deep at the center of your being."

"If we don't know life, how can we know death?"

"Life is really simple, but we insist on making it complicated."

"Old age, believe me, is a good and pleasant thing. It is true you are gently shouldered off the stage, but then you are given such a comfortable front stall as spectator."

"Speak the truth, do not yield to anger; give, if thou art asked for little; by these three steps thou wilt go near the gods."

"Study the past, if you would define the future."

"The more man meditates upon good thoughts, the better will be his world and the world at large."

"The Path is not far from man. When men try to pursue a course, which is far from the common indications of consciousness, this course cannot be considered The Path."

"The superior man does what is proper to the station in which he is; he does not desire to go beyond this. In a position of wealth and honor, he does what is proper to a position of wealth and honor. In a poor and low position, he does what is proper to a poor and low position."

"The superior man honors his virtuous nature, and maintains constant inquiry and study, seeking to carry it out to its breadth and greatness, so as to omit none of the more exquisite and minute points which it embraces, and to raise it to its greatest height and brilliancy."

"The way of the superior man may be compared to what takes place in traveling, when to go to a distance we must first traverse the space that is near, and in ascending a height, when we must begin from the lower ground."

"There are three things which the superior man guards against. In youth … lust. When he is strong … quarrelsomeness. When he is old … covetousness."

"What you do not want done to yourself, do not do to others."

"When one cultivates to the utmost the principles of his nature, and exercises them on the principle of reciprocity, he is not far from the path."

"When the Superior Man eats he does not try to stuff himself; at rest he does not seek perfect comfort; he is diligent in his work and careful in speech. He avails himself to people of the Tao and thereby corrects himself. This is the kind of person of whom you can say, 'he loves learning.'"

"When you are laboring for others let it be with the same zeal as if it were for yourself."

Humility

"A superior man is modest in his speech, but exceeds in his actions."

"He who speaks without modesty will find it difficult to make his words good."

"The superior man is distressed by the limitations of his ability; he is not distressed by the fact that men do not recognize the ability that he has."

Influence

"All things are nourished together without their injuring one another. The courses of the seasons, and of the sun and moon, are pursued without any collision among them. The smaller energies are like river currents; the greater energies are seen in mighty transformations. It is this which makes heaven and earth so great."

"Among the appliances to transform the people, sound and appearances are but trivial influences."

"Sincerity becomes apparent. From being apparent, it becomes manifest. From being manifest, it becomes brilliant. Brilliant, it affects others. Affecting others, they are changed by it. Changed by it, they are transformed. It is only he who is possessed of the most complete sincerity that can exist under heaven, who can transform."

Intelligence

"When we have intelligence resulting from sincerity, this condition is to be ascribed to nature; when we have sincerity resulting from intelligence, this condition is to be ascribed to instruction. But given the sincerity, and there shall be the intelligence; given the intelligence, and there shall be the sincerity."

Knowledge and Learning

"By three methods we may learn wisdom: First, by reflection, which is noblest; Second, by imitation, which is easiest; and third by experience, which is the bitterest."

"He who learns but does not think, is lost! He who thinks but does not learn is in great danger."

"I am not one who was born in the possession of knowledge; I am one who is fond of antiquity, and earnest in seeking it there."

"If you think in terms of a year, plant a seed; if in terms of ten years, plant trees; if in terms of 100 years, teach the people."

"Ignorance is the night of the mind, but a night without moon and star."

"Learn as though you would never be able to master it; Hold it as though you would be in fear of losing it."

"Learning without thought is labor lost; thought without learning is perilous."

"Real knowledge is to know the extent of one's ignorance."

"Reviewing what you have learned and learning anew, you are fit to be a teacher."

"The scholar who cherishes the love of comfort is not fit to be deemed a scholar."

"Things have their root and their branches. Affairs have their end and their beginning. To know what is first and what is last will lead near to what is taught in the Great Learning."

"To be fond of learning is to be near to knowledge. To practice with vigor is to be near to magnanimity. To possess the feeling of shame is to be near to energy."

"To study and not think is a waste. To think and not study is dangerous."

"When you know a thing, to hold that you know it, and when you do not know a thing, to allow that you do not know it – this is knowledge."

"You cannot open a book without learning something."

Personal Development

"The will to win, the desire to succeed, the urge to reach your full potential… these are the keys that will unlock the door to personal excellence."

"When we see men of worth, we should think of equaling them; when we see men of a contrary character, we should turn inwards and examine ourselves."

"When you meet someone better than yourself, turn your thoughts to becoming his equal. When you meet someone not as good as you are, look within and examine your own self."

Revenge

"Before you embark on a journey of revenge, dig two graves."

Truth

"The object of the superior man is truth."

"The superior man does not set his mind either for anything, or against anything; what is right he will follow."

"The superior man, even when he is not moving, has a feeling of reverence, and while he speaks not, he has the feeling of truthfulness."

"They who know the truth are not equal to those who love it, and they who love it are not equal to those who delight in it."

Uniqueness

"The way of Heaven and Earth may be completely declared in one sentence: They are without any doubleness, and so they produce things in a manner that is unfathomable."

Virtue

"Fine words and an insinuating appearance are seldom associated with true virtue."

"Go before the people with your example, and be laborious in their affairs."

"I have not seen a person who loved virtue, or one who hated what was not virtuous. He who loved virtue would esteem nothing above it."

"Is virtue a thing remote? I wish to be virtuous, and lo! Virtue is at hand."

"The determined scholar and the man of virtue will not seek to live at the expense of injuring their virtue. They will even sacrifice their lives to preserve their virtue complete."

"The firm, the enduring, the simple, and the modest are near to virtue."

"The man of virtue makes the difficulty to be overcome his first interest; success only comes later."

"The superior man thinks always of virtue; the common man thinks of comfort."

"The virtuous man is driven by responsibility, the non-virtuous man is driven by profit."

"Virtue is more to man than either water or fire. I have seen men die from treading on water and fire, but I have never seen a man die from treading the course of virtue."

"Virtue is not left to stand alone. He who practices it will have neighbors."

"Virtuous people often revenge themselves for the constraints to which they submit by the boredom which they inspire."

"What the great learning teaches, is to illustrate illustrious virtue; to renovate the people; and to rest in the highest excellence."
"When a man's knowledge is sufficient to attain, and his virtue is not sufficient to enable him to hold, whatever he may have gained, he will lose again."

Also by Daniel Willey:

365 Fun, Uplifting, Motivating, and Inspirational Quotes You've Never Heard Before

365 Fun, Uplifting, and Inspirational Quotes from all the Top Movies

Be Great: 365 Inspirational Quotes from the World's Most Influential People

Success Isn't For Everyone: How to Build the Foundation for a Successful Future

The Top 365 Fun, Uplifting, Motivating, and Inspirational Quotes of all Time

Daily Love Quotes

The Teachings of Gandhi

About The Author

Daniel Willey became interested in books at a very young age. His mother was a huge advocate of reading and would regularly hold 'read-a-thons' for the family. Daniel graduated from the University of Utah in Emergency Medicine. He spent two years as a missionary in Thailand and has a great love for the country and people there. Daniel is currently writing another book and says that he has several ideas for more books "in the pipeline." He enjoys playing his two favorite instruments, the piano and bagpipes.

Looking to get Published?

Visit us at: http://www.easypublishingcompany.com
and mention this ad for 10% off!

CPSIA information can be obtained at www.ICGtesting.com
Printed in the USA
LVOW11s0921170716

496666LV00003B/479/P